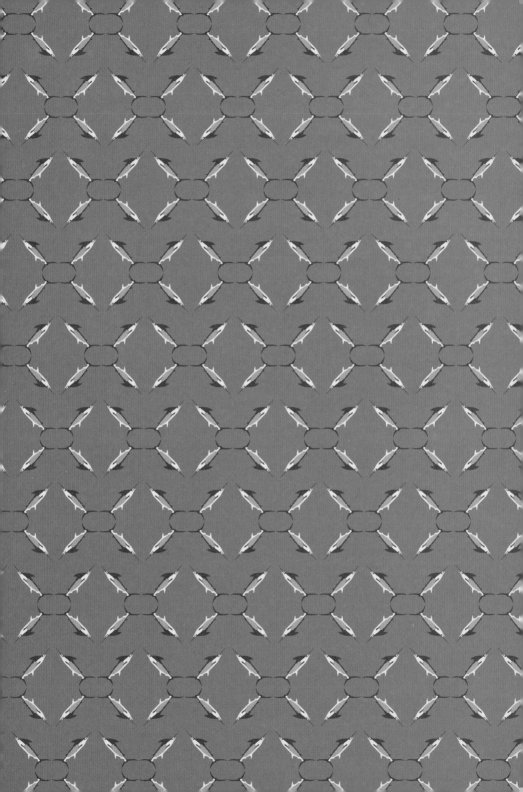

BIOGRAPHIC
HEMINGWAY

BIOGRAPHIC
HEMINGWAY

JAMIE PUMFREY

AMMONITE
PRESS

First published 2019 by
Ammonite Press
an imprint of Guild of Master Craftsman Publications Ltd
Castle Place, 166 High Street, Lewes, East Sussex, BN7 1XU,
United Kingdom
www.ammonitepress.com

ISBN 978 1 78145 343 8

A catalogue record for this book is available from the
British Library.

Publisher: Jason Hook
Concept Design: Matt Carr
Design & Illustration: Matt Carr & Robin Shields
Editor: Judith Chamberlain-Webber

Colour reproduction by GMC Reprographics
Printed and bound in Turkey

CONTENTS

ICONOGRAPHIC

WHEN WE CAN RECOGNIZE A WRITER BY A SET OF ICONS, WE CAN ALSO RECOGNIZE HOW COMPLETELY THAT WRITER AND THEIR WORK HAVE ENTERED OUR CULTURE AND OUR CONSCIOUSNESS.

INTRODUCTION

Writer, novelist, journalist, editor, war correspondent, poet, playwright, ambulance driver, war hero, big-game hunter, deep-sea fisherman, Nobel and Pulitzer Prize winner, drinker, musician, boxer, skier, sailor, playboy, friend of Roosevelt and Castro, enemy of Franco, member of The Lost Generation: Ernest Hemingway was all of these and more.

Driven by a deep-seated need for adventure, Hemingway was a man of action – be it on the frontlines of war dodging (or not dodging) bullets and bombs, or on his fishing boat hunting sharks and German U-boats. Using these experiences as the basis for his novels, along with an evocative and engaging journalistic style of writing, he captured the imagination of the public and became both a commercial and critical success.

"THE WORLD BREAKS EVERY ONE AND AFTERWARD MANY ARE STRONG AT THE BROKEN PLACES."

—Ernest Hemingway,
A Farewell to Arms, 1929

Hemingway grew up in Chicago, Illinois, and was encouraged by his parents to be creative and adventurous. He played the cello and could shoot and fish. In the classroom he showed a natural flair for the English language, and on the playing field he discovered a love of boxing that would continue throughout his life. His first job out of high school was as a newspaper reporter, and it was there that he learnt how to write with the succinct prose – devoid of adjectives – that would become his signature style. Just six months later, though, he left to pursue naïve dreams of heroism in the First World War. After being injured in Italy, he returned home a changed man – his experiences of death and destruction would forever shape his view on the world.

But it was France that really transformed Hemingway from the ordinary to the extraordinary. He married Hadley Richardson in September 1921 and, four months later, the couple settled in the Latin Quarter of Paris. Hemingway's recollections of his early years in Europe tell of poverty and desperation, but in truth they lived quite comfortably. Due to the economic consequences of war, Paris was inexpensive for foreigners, and he was surrounded by expatriates from the USA, including the writers F. Scott Fitzgerald and Gertrude Stein. Feeling disillusioned with life in post-war society and struggling to find an identity, they described themselves as 'The Lost Generation', but from this struggle came great art and literature. Encouraged by Stein, and directly influenced by artists such as Pablo Picasso and the poet Ezra Pound, Hemingway began working on the fiction that would make him a household name.

Married four times, Hemingway struggled with the routine of daily life and he rarely spent much time in one location. "Writing and travel broaden your ass if not your mind," he wrote in 1950 and the global experiences he had encountered throughout his lifetime, both as a war correspondent and in his personal life, affected his writing. In Spain, he saw bullfighting and lived through the Spanish Civil War (*The Sun Also Rises* and *For Whom the Bell Tolls*). In France, he reported on two World Wars and helped liberate Paris from the Nazis (*Across the River and into the Trees* and *A Moveable Feast*). In Cuba, he made friends with revolutionaries and won the Nobel and Pulitzer prizes (*The Old Man and the Sea*). And in Africa, he hunted big game and was involved in two plane crashes (*Green Hills of Africa*).

In his final years, Hemingway's reckless behaviour began to catch up with him. He suffered ongoing pain from ancient injuries – nine concussions, bullet wounds, broken bones and ruptured organs – as well as from mental illness. To treat his depression he undertook a treatment of electroconvulsive therapy, which in turn destroyed his memory and he found it impossible to write. His depression worsened and just like his father before him, and later two of his siblings, Hemingway committed suicide.

There are two sides to the Hemingway coin. One is the hard-drinking womanizer, a red-blooded man's man who enjoyed bullfighting, hunting and boxing, becoming a literary icon and a 20th-century hero. The other is the fragile, insecure writer who suffered from addiction and mental illness. A serial adulterer, he pushed away his family and fell out with his friends. Legends are often based on truth but, over time, they become embellished. Ever the storyteller, Hemingway helped blur the lines between fact and fiction in the name of a great narrative. But, as you examine the extraordinary life of one of the finest of American authors, it's hard to see why he needed to bother.

"THE MOST COMPLICATED SUBJECT THAT I KNOW, SINCE I AM A MAN, IS A MAN'S LIFE."

—Ernest Hemingway, *The Christmas Gift*, *Look* magazine, 1954

ERNEST HEMINGWAY

01
LIFE

"THE GOOD PARTS OF A BOOK MAY BE ONLY SOMETHING A WRITER IS LUCKY ENOUGH TO OVERHEAR OR IT MAY BE THE WRECK OF HIS WHOLE DAMN LIFE — AND ONE IS AS GOOD AS THE OTHER."

—Ernest Hemingway, in a letter to
F. Scott Fitzgerald, 1929

ERNEST MILLER HEMINGWAY

was born 21 July 1899 in Oak Park, Illinois, USA

Ernest was the second of six children born to Clarence Edmonds Hemingway, a medical practitioner, and Grace Hall, a musician and artist. The Hemingways were well educated and highly respected, staunch patriots who upheld traditional Christian values – the embodiment of the American middle class.

Despite the highly autobiographical nature of his work, Hemingway wrote little about his childhood. Each summer, the family vacationed at a cabin on Walloon Lake in northern Michigan, USA, where Clarence encouraged the young Ernest to hunt and fish. At home, he was taught to play the cello by his mother and would perform concerts with his siblings. Though he had talent and spent many hours practising, he felt detached from the music and confessed that his mind would wander and start formulating the stories that would later make him famous.

OAK PARK

Just 9 miles (15km) west of downtown Chicago, Oak Park was an attractive village with an intensely conservative community. The Hemingway's house, an expansive Victorian property built in 1890, was the first in the suburb to have electricity.

....

Also born in Oak Park – FRANK LLOYD WRIGHT (1867–1959), architect and designer. There are 25 buildings designed by Lloyd Wright in the Oak Park region of Illinois, the largest collection of his work anywhere in the world.

....

ILLINOIS

USA

The Spanish–American War formally ends.

ENGLAND

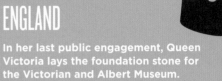

In her last public engagement, Queen Victoria lays the foundation stone for the Victorian and Albert Museum.

CUBA

The end of Spanish rule in Cuba.

FRANCE

A radio signal is transmitted across the English Channel for the first time by Guglielmo Marconi.

SOUTH AFRICA

The start of the Second Boer War.

THE WORLD IN 1899

RUSSIA

Leo Tolstoy finishes his last novel, *Resurrection*.

Hemingway was born at the conclusion of the 19th century, a period of rapid urbanization, scientific discovery and technological growth around the world. Significant developments in the fields of physics and mathematics had transformed electrical science from mere curiosity into an essential part of modern life. In Europe, improved standards of living had more than doubled the population, from 200 million to more than 400 million. Meanwhile, on the other side of the Atlantic, large-scale farming, international trade and the expansion of the rail system had established the USA as a world power. The Spanish-American War in 1898 had ended with the collapse of the Spanish empire and the USA took temporary control of Cuba, Puerto Rico, the Pacific island of Guam and the Philippines. At the turn of the century, the stage was set for a fraught and fragile period of economic, social and cultural change.

NETHERLANDS

The First Hague Convention is signed.

PHILIPPINES

The Philippine–American War begins in Manila.

AUSTRALIA

Cyclone Mahina strikes Queensland, killing more than 300 people. It is the deadliest cyclone in Australian history.

HEMINGWAY'S FAMILY TREE

GRANDFATHER
Anson Tyler
Hemingway
(1844–1926)

GRANDMOTHER
Adelaide Edmonds
Hemingway
(1841–1923)

FATHER
Clarence Edmonds
Hemingway
(1871–1928)

SISTER
Marcelline
Hemingway
(1898–1963)

**Ernest Miller
Hemingway**
(1899–1961)

SISTER
Ursula
Hemingway
(1902–66)

FIRST WIFE
Elizabeth Hadley
Richardson
(1891–1979)

SECOND WIFE
Pauline Marie
Pfeiffer
(1895–1951)

SON
John Hadley
Nicanor 'Jack'
Hemingway
(1923–2000)

SON
Patrick Miller
Hemingway
(b. 1928)

SON
Gregory Hancock
Hemingway
(1931–2001)

Having been friends at school, Ernest's parents were reacquainted in 1895 when Clarence, the local physician, cared for Grace's mother in the last year of her life. The couple quickly became romantically involved, and Grace sacrificed the opportunity to train as an opera singer in New York, USA, to continue the relationship. In 1896, the couple married and two years later the first of their six children was born.

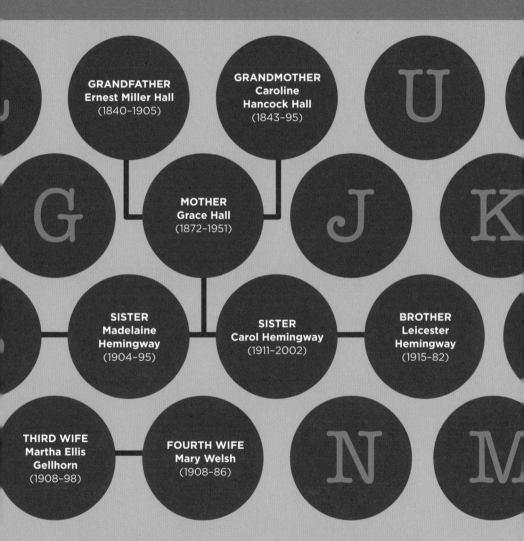

GRANDFATHER
Ernest Miller Hall
(1840–1905)

GRANDMOTHER
Caroline
Hancock Hall
(1843–95)

MOTHER
Grace Hall
(1872–1951)

SISTER
Madelaine
Hemingway
(1904–95)

SISTER
Carol Hemingway
(1911–2002)

BROTHER
Leicester
Hemingway
(1915–82)

THIRD WIFE
Martha Ellis
Gellhorn
(1908–98)

FOURTH WIFE
Mary Welsh
(1908–86)

For a time, the family was happy, but Clarence became depressed after a series of poor financial investments and ongoing health issues. He committed suicide when his youngest son, Leicester, was just 13 years old. After her husband's death, Grace became a successful painter – creating more than 600 works of art – and a campaigner for women's rights. Initially, Ernest offered Grace financial support. But after each blamed the other for Clarence's death, the relationship turned sour, and Hemingway later refused to attend his mother's funeral.

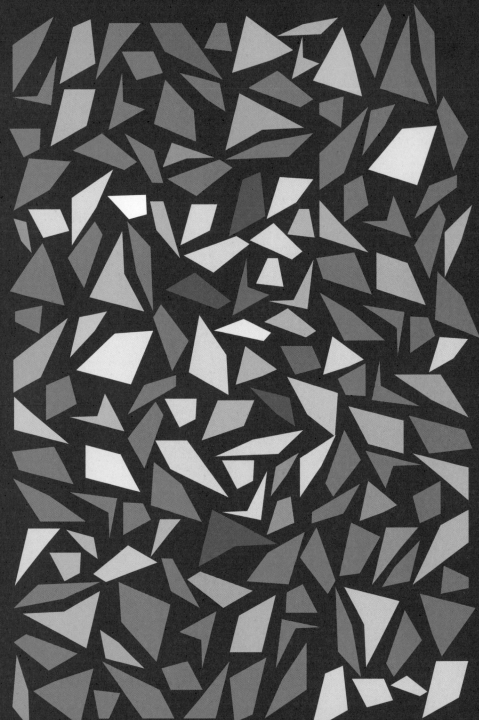

HEMINGWAY SUFFERED 227 SHRAPNEL WOUNDS IN THE FIRST WORLD WAR

In December 1917, at just 18 years old, Hemingway attempted to enlist in the US Army but was rejected due to a hereditary defect in his left eye. Determined to experience action in the First World War, he volunteered with the American Red Cross as an ambulance driver for the Italian Army and seven months later was in Paris.

Hemingway spent only a few days in France before he was relocated to the small town of Schio in northern Italy. On 8 July 1918, just two weeks before his 19th birthday, Hemingway was running chocolate to soldiers in the trenches when the town was hit by mortar fire. He was badly wounded, receiving more than 200 shrapnel wounds to his legs. Remarkably, Hemingway was able to get clear, carrying an injured soldier away from the immediate danger, despite being struck again by enemy bullets. He was one of the first Americans to be wounded in Italy in the war and received the Silver Medal of Military Valor for his bravery. His time in Italy, including six months recovering in an Italian hospital and a failed romance with an American nurse, served as the inspiration for Hemingway's 1929 novel, *A Farewell to Arms.*

LIFE ON THE MOVE

1920
Moves to Toronto and begins freelancing for the *Toronto Star Weekly* magazine.

1920

Heads to Chicago and takes a job as a writer for the *Cooperative Commonwealth* journal.

1921
Meets Hadley Richardson while she is visiting friends in Chicago. After months of correspondence, they marry on 3 September in Horton Bay, Michigan.

1923

Having filed 95 reports over 20 months in Europe, Hemingway returns to Toronto. His first son, John Hadley, is born in October.

1923

Hemingway and Ezra Pound take a walking tour of Italy.

1922
Reports on the Greco-Turkish war and the aftermath of the Great Fire of Smyrna.

1922
Employed as a foreign correspondent for the *Toronto Star* and moves to Paris, where he meets writers including Gertrude Stein, James Joyce and Ezra Pound.

 CANADA

USA

 TURKEY

FRANCE

ITALY

SPAIN

SWITZERLAND

CUBA

BAHAMAS

1924

Resigns from the *Toronto Star Weekly* and moves to Paris.

Works on the monthly literary journal, *The Transatlantic Review*.

1926

Travels south to Provence, Nîmes, Arles, Avignon, Les Baux and St-Rémy.

1927

Divorces Hadley. Hemingway offers her the proceeds from *The Sun Also Rises* as part of the settlement. He spends the winter skiing in Gstaad, and in May he marries Pauline Pfeiffer.

1928

Leaves Paris for Key West, Florida. In June, his second son, Patrick, is born. Clarence Hemingway commits suicide in December.

1929

Attends the Festival of San Fermín in Pamplona, Spain, for the sixth time. The trip will form the basis for his next book, *Death in the Afternoon*.

1934

Buys a boat, *Pilar*, and learns to sail in the Caribbean.

1931

Returns to the US for the birth of his third son, Gregory.

1932

Visits Cuba on a fishing expedition with friends.

1937

Travels to Spain to cover the Spanish Civil War for the North American Newspaper Alliance and begins a relationship with Martha Gellhorn.

RELATIONSHIPS BY NUMBERS

Hemingway had a female companion for more than 40 years of his life, but the relationships were characterized by tension, torment and ultimately betrayal. He had four marriages and was unfaithful in each. While married to his first wife, Hadley Richardson, Hemingway began a relationship with journalist Pauline Pfeiffer, even inviting Pauline on the couple's family holidays. He would repeat this pattern in his second and third marriages. In his memoir *A Moveable Feast*, Hemingway reminisced fondly about his relationship with Hadley, and even attempted to take responsibility for a number of the issues that caused the breakdown of the marriage, but ultimately portrayed himself as the victim. The wives of Hemingway were all attractive, intelligent and determined women. They were each extraordinary in their own way and were always more than just 'Mrs Hemingway'.

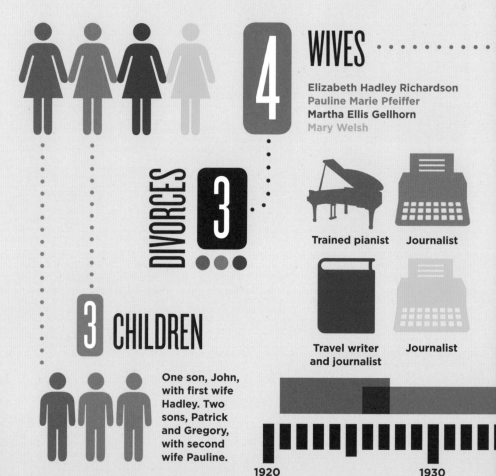

4 WIVES

Elizabeth Hadley Richardson
Pauline Marie Pfeiffer
Martha Ellis Gellhorn
Mary Welsh

3 DIVORCES

Trained pianist

Journalist

Travel writer and journalist

Journalist

3 CHILDREN

One son, John, with first wife Hadley. Two sons, Patrick and Gregory, with second wife Pauline.

1920   1930

7 MONTHS SPENT NOT MARRIED IN 40 YEARS

3 HOMES

After renting apartments in Paris with Hadley and Pauline, as Hemingway became more successful he purchased homes in Florida, Havana and Idaho.

AMERICAN BORN

Hadley and Martha were both born in St Louis, Missouri; Pauline in Parkersburg, Iowa; and Mary in Walker, Minnesota.

The Sun Also Rises

Death in the Afternoon

For Whom the Bell Tolls

Across the River and into the Trees

HEMINGWAY DEDICATED A BOOK TO EACH OF HIS WIVES

RELATIONSHIPS TIMELINE

Hemingway met Hadley in 1921 and a year later they were married. After five years, he started an affair with Pauline Pfeiffer and, in May 1927, she became his second wife. While reporting on the Spanish Civil War, Hemingway began an affair with Martha Gellhorn and, after his divorce from Pauline was finalized, the two were married. The relationship eventually broke down, and Hemingway started a relationship with Mary Welsh while both were still married to other people.

1940   1950   1960

CHEATING DEATH

In 1954, while sightseeing in Uganda, Africa, Hemingway and his wife Mary were involved in two near-fatal plane crashes. The first incident occurred when their plane had to make an emergency landing. Having survived somewhat unscathed, they were collected by the Royal Air Force, but shortly after takeoff, just 48 hours after their first crash, the plane nosedived into the ground. Both were seriously injured, although not quite badly enough to warrant the many newspaper headlines that prematurely reported their deaths. Surprisingly, the Hemingways accepted an offer of a third flight out of Africa.

FIRST CRASH

DATE: 23 January 1954

CAUSE: Caught an abandoned telegraph wire, while flying at low altitude to avoid hitting a flock of white ibis.

RECOVERY: After landing in heavy foliage, the couple and their pilot spent the night in the bush before a passing tourist boat, which had been previously used in the 1951 film *The African Queen*, eventually rescued them.

INJURIES: Mary broke 2 ribs; Ernest injured his spine, arm and shoulder.

$20,000 Paid by *Look* magazine for an exclusive about the plane crashes. The piece, written by Hemingway, ran across 20 pages over two issues.

Single-engine Cessna 180

HEMINGWAY SURVIVES TWO PLANE CRASHES IN 48 HOURS!

CRASH 1

Murchison Falls National Park, Uganda

CRASH 2

Butiaba, Uganda

SECOND CRASH

DATE: 25 January 1954

CAUSE: During take-off, the wheels got caught on an anthill and bushes at the end of the runway, causing the plane to nosedive.

RECOVERY: Mary and the pilot escaped unharmed through a window, but Hemingway, too large to fit through the gap, was trapped in the wreckage. He escaped by headbutting the door, lacerating his scalp, shortly before the plane caught fire.

INJURIES: Ernest suffered a ruptured kidney, spleen and liver; a sprained arm and leg; crushed vertebrae; a fractured skull; a paralyzed sphincter; first-degree burns; a lacerated scalp; and the temporary loss of hearing and eyesight.

De Havilland DH.89 Dragon Rapide

MAN OF THE WORLD

1941 Travels to China to report on the Second Sino-Japanese war.

1952 *The Old Man and the Sea* is published in full in *Life* magazine. It goes on to win the Pulitzer Prize for Fiction.

1939 Moves to Cuba with Martha Gellhorn. The couple rent a room at the Hotel Ambos Mundos before purchasing a farmhouse 12 miles (19 km) outside of Havana.

1945 Hemingway and Gellhorn divorce. The following year, Hemingway marries Mary Welsh and she moves to Cuba.

1935

1940

1945

1950

For his journalism in the war, Hemingway is awarded a Bronze Star.

1940 With his divorce from Pauline confirmed, Hemingway and Martha marry in Cheyenne, Wyoming, USA.

1947

1944 Works as a foreign correspondent during the Second World War and is present at the Liberation of Paris. Meets Mary Welsh.

CHINA

USA

FRANCE

SPAIN

CUBA

UGANDA

SWEDEN

1956 Discovers two trunks left at the Ritz Paris filled with his early writings. They form the basis for what will become *A Moveable Feast*.

1960 Leaves Cuba and moves to New York City before settling in Ketchum.

1959 Spends the summer in Spain watching bullfighting. The trip forms the basis of his final book *The Dangerous Summer*, published posthumously in 1985.

1953 Goes on safari. In 1954, he is injured in successive plane crashes.

1955

1960

1965

1954 Receives the Nobel Prize in Literature "for his mastery of the art of narrative, most recently demonstrated in *The Old Man and the Sea,* and for the influence that he has exerted on contemporary style."

1959 Buys a large house and 17 acres (7 ha) of land in Ketchum, Idaho, for $50,000.

1961 Suffering from depression, Hemingway undergoes electroconvulsive therapy. Two days after a final round of treatment, he commits suicide.

9 CONCUSSIONS

57 STITCHES

Hemingway lacerated his scalp being thrown through the windscreen of his car during a crash.

TEMPORARY LOSS OF VISION IN RIGHT EYE

9 STITCHES

Required after he accidently pulled a skylight down onto his head in Paris. It left him with a permanent scar on his forehead.

- ● WOUND
- ○ BURN
- ● FRACTURE
- ● ORGAN RUPTURE
- ● INFECTION/ILLNESS
- ● MUSCLE INJURY
- ● OTHER

TINNITUS

RUPTURED KIDNEY

RUPTURED SPLEEN

SHOT THROUGH TESTICLE

BULLET WOUNDS

Self-inflicted while trying to shoot sharks off Key West.

THE SURVIVOR

"In order to write about life, first you must live it," Hemingway once said. And, true to his word, he did. He took risks, he was impulsive and he never shied away from a challenge. Even being wounded during the First World War, Hemingway saw as a positive experience. His medical history is testament to his attitude or, perhaps, exposes him as someone who was just plain unlucky.

227 SHRAPNEL WOUNDS

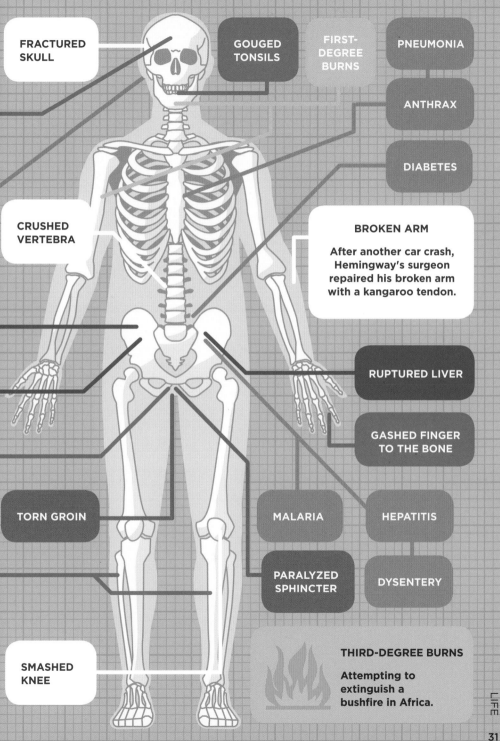

FRACTURED SKULL

GOUGED TONSILS

FIRST-DEGREE BURNS

PNEUMONIA

ANTHRAX

DIABETES

CRUSHED VERTEBRA

BROKEN ARM

After another car crash, Hemingway's surgeon repaired his broken arm with a kangaroo tendon.

RUPTURED LIVER

GASHED FINGER TO THE BONE

TORN GROIN

MALARIA

HEPATITIS

PARALYZED SPHINCTER

DYSENTERY

SMASHED KNEE

THIRD-DEGREE BURNS

Attempting to extinguish a bushfire in Africa.

THE DEATH OF HEMINGWAY

Hemingway was 61 years old when he died from a self-inflicted gunshot wound to the head. Just two days before, he had been released from a final session of electroconvulsive therapy, designed to provide relief from chronic depression. He had also suffered much physical pain and discomfort in the previous few years – caused by a number of serious injuries finally catching up with him. This, coupled with the electroconvulsive therapy, led to an inability to think clearly and writing became impossible. When asked to provide some words for John F. Kennedy's inauguration, Hemingway struggled to compose even a single sentence.

This failure, in turn, triggered a deeper depression. In April 1961, Mary found Hemingway sitting in the kitchen with a shotgun and two shells, and later he was discovered attempting to walk into the propellers of a moving plane. Three months later she awoke to discover his body near the back door – a double-barrelled, 12-gauge shotgun beside him.

DATE:
2 JULY 1961

AGE:
61

CAUSE OF DEATH:
SUICIDE

Hemingway was buried in Ketchum Cemetery, Idaho, USA, and his family erected a memorial in 1966. His epitaph (below) is taken from a friend's eulogy that he wrote in 1939.

"IF I CAN'T LIVE ON MY OWN TERMS, THEN EXISTENCE IS IMPOSSIBLE."

—Ernest Hemingway, June 1961

"BEST OF ALL HE LOVED THE FALL
THE LEAVES YELLOW ON THE COTTONWOODS
LEAVES FLOATING ON THE TROUT STREAMS
AND ABOVE THE HILLS
          THE HIGH BLUE WINDLESS SKIES
...NOW HE WILL BE A PART OF THEM FOREVER
          ERNEST HEMINGWAY – IDAHO – 1939

THERE HAVE BEEN 5 SUICIDES OVER 4 GENERATIONS OF THE HEMINGWAY FAMILY

5

ERNEST HEMINGWAY

02
WORLD

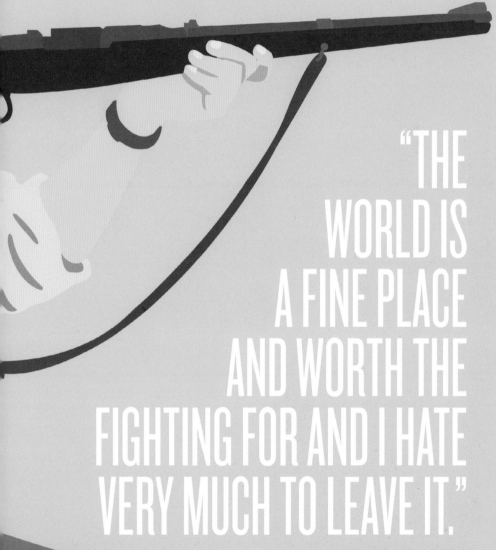

"THE
WORLD IS
A FINE PLACE
AND WORTH THE
FIGHTING FOR AND I HATE
VERY MUCH TO LEAVE IT."

—Ernest Hemingway, *For Whom the Bell Tolls*, 1940

HEMINGWAY'S PARIS

Paris is as much a part of Hemingway as Hemingway is a part of Paris. "If you are lucky enough to have lived in Paris as a young man," Hemingway once wrote, "then wherever you go for the rest of your life, it stays with you, for Paris is a moveable feast." And Hemingway was a young man, just 22, when he first arrived. After the austerity of the First World War, Paris became the cultural capital of the world – art, architecture, music, literature and fashion all flourished. The city had such an impact on him that Hemingway's final work was a memoir so detailed – in so few words – that you can almost feel your feet on the cobbles of rue du Cardinal Lemoine, where he first lived, as you read it. *A Moveable Feast*, published posthumously in 1964, was Hemingway's love letter to Paris – a romanticized portrait of Bohemian bliss.

HOMES

1   74 rue du Cardinal Lemoine
With first wife, Hadley (1922–23)

2   113 rue Notre-Dame-des-Champs
With Hadley (1924–26)

3   69 rue Froidevaux
With second wife, Pauline (1927)

4   6 rue Férou
With Pauline (1927–28)

RECREATION

5 39 rue Descartes
Hemingway rented the top floor as an office.

6 SHAKESPEARE AND COMPANY
12 rue de l'Odéon
Meeting place for aspiring writers, including Hemingway, James Joyce and F. Scott Fitzgerald.

7 27 rue de Fleurus
Home of Gertrude Stein, who was a patron of artist Pablo Picasso and mentor to Hemingway.

8 MUSÉE DU LUXEMBOURG
19 rue de Vaugirard
Hemingway frequently visited to observe the paintings of Monet and Cézanne.

CAFÉS

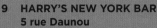

9 HARRY'S NEW YORK BAR
5 rue Daunou
Home of the Bloody Mary, and a favourite spot for American expats.

10 THE RITZ BAR
38 rue Cambon
It is said that Hemingway drank 51 dry martinis here during the Liberation of Paris. In 1994, it was renamed The Hemingway Bar.

11 LE SELECT
99 boulevard du Montparnasse
Hemingway wrote the café into his debut novel *The Sun Also Rises*.

12 LA CLOSERIE DES LILAS
171 boulevard du Montparnasse
In the morning, Hemingway would sit on the terrace, writing. In the afternoons, he was at the bar, drinking. He wrote some of *The Sun Also Rises* here.

13 LE DINGO
10 rue Delambre
Hemingway first met F. Scott Fitzgerald here.

14 MICHAUD'S
29 rue des Saints-Pères
When times were good, Hemingway ate well at this restaurant. It was also a favourite of author James Joyce.

5

1

THE LOST GENERATION

Coined by author and poet Gertrude Stein, and later appropriated by Hemingway in *The Sun Also Rises*, the term 'Une Génération Perdue' ('A Lost Generation') defined the writers, poets, artists and musicians of 1920s' Paris who felt disillusioned with life in post-war society. The First World War had devastated Europe and many questioned traditional values such as honour and modesty, instead favouring recklessness and excess. But, while the world felt uncomfortable to them, The Lost Generation recognized that they were living in a time of great change and found hope in a future that they could shape. Their impact on the arts in the 20th century cannot be overstated.

| **Ernest Hemingway** | **Pablo Picasso** | **F. Scott Fitzgerald** | **Max Jacob** |
| (1899–1961) | (1881-1973) | (1896-1940) | (1876–1944) |

| **Juan Gris** | **Georges Braque** | **Henri Matisse** | **James Joyce** |
| (1887–1927) | (1882–1963) | (1869-1954) | (1882–1941) |

● WRITER
● POET
● ARTIST
● DANCER

38 PICASSOS OWNED BY GERTRUDE STEIN

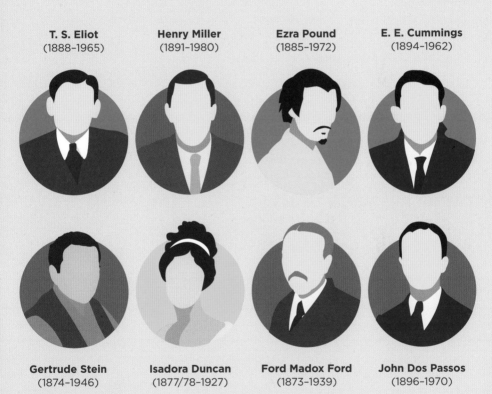

T. S. Eliot
(1888–1965)

Henry Miller
(1891–1980)

Ezra Pound
(1885–1972)

E. E. Cummings
(1894–1962)

Gertrude Stein
(1874–1946)

Isadora Duncan
(1877/78–1927)

Ford Madox Ford
(1873–1939)

John Dos Passos
(1896–1970)

27 RUE DE FLEURUS

Gertrude Stein's weekly salons were held at 27 rue de Fleurus, where key figures in literature and art came together to appreciate and critique. Stein is often referred to as the mother of The Lost Generation and the paintings of Picasso and Matisse and the writings of James Joyce and F. Scott Fitzgerald would not exist without her guiding hand. Stein had a turbulent relationship with Hemingway; once his mentor and the godmother to his son John, she was later a target for humiliation and cruelty in his novels.

REPORTS FROM THE FRONTLINE

Although he is remembered for his fiction, Hemingway initially built his career through his war reports, which were unique in committing to telling the truth above all else. Ensuring that he was always on the frontlines, Hemingway never censored the horrific realities of life on the battlefield. In 1942, *Men at War*, an anthology of war stories edited and introduced by Hemingway, was published. The project was intended to provide inspiration and justification for US involvement in the Second World War. Two years later, as the conflict reached its climax, Hemingway spent ten months in England and France reporting on the fighting. Despite the risks, he was present at many significant events, including the D-Day landings and the Liberation of Paris. His experiences during the war affected him deeply, and would become a central theme in numerous key works.

FIRST WORLD WAR (1914–18)

Hemingway's participation in the First World War ended with him being hospitalized. His experience of the war was referenced in two short stories, *Soldier's Home* and *Big Two-Hearted River*, and one novel, *A Farewell to Arms*.

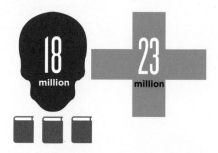

18 million

23 million

GRECO-TURKISH WAR (1919–22)

Before becoming a published author, Hemingway travelled to Turkey in 1922 as a correspondent for the *Toronto Star Weekly* to cover the Greco-Turkish War. In total he wrote 20 articles on the conflict.

200,000

Turkey

125,000

Greece

500,000

Turkey

1.5 million

Greece

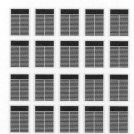

SPANISH CIVIL WAR (1936–39)

1 million

500,000

Hemingway reported on the hostilities (penning 31 dispatches); wrote a pro-Republican propaganda film, *The Spanish Earth*; raised money for the Spanish ambulance fund; and wrote a play, *The Fifth Column*. His experiences provided the inspiration for his 1940 novel *For Whom the Bell Tolls*.

26 million

95 million

SECOND SINO-JAPANESE WAR (1937–45)

Hemingway's only visit to Asia occurred on assignment for *PM* magazine to report on the Second Sino-Japanese War. During the trip, he failed to find any of the fighting.

SECOND WORLD WAR (1939–45)

In 1944, Hemingway left Cuba for Europe to report on the Second World War. Stopping in London, he was seriously injured in a car accident. In France, he wrote seven articles for *Collier's* magazine and his 1950 novel, *Across the River and into the Trees*, is regarded as Hemingway's response to the atrocities he saw.

70–85 million

3% of the world's population

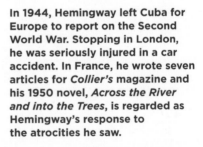

● DEAD

✚ WOUNDED

🧳 REFUGEES

When he wasn't writing, or propping up the bar, Hemingway was often found with a rod or rifle in his hand. By the age of three he knew how to fish and could handle a gun. A year later he was accompanying his father on hunting expeditions. In later life, he found a passion for big-game hunting in Africa and deep-water fishing, taking his boat, *Pilar*, out to hook marlin and tuna. The years spent in the Caribbean allowed Hemingway's skills as an angler to flourish and, in 1935, he won every competition between Key West in Florida, Havana in Cuba and Bimini in the Bahamas. While living in Havana, he organized an annual marlin-fishing contest (now called the Ernest Hemingway International Billfishing Tournament), winning the first three events. In 1960, Fidel Castro, Prime Minister of Cuba, took home the title. Ever the competitor, Hemingway focused not so much on the kill, but on the thrill of the hunt – man against beast.

$20,000
Cost of an African safari in 1930

35 HYENAS
Shot following the wildebeest migration

HUNTING
AND FISHING

7 MARLIN
Caught in a single day, a world record in 1938

"I HAVE TWO WELL DEVELOPED TALENTS; FOR SEA FISHING ... AND SHOOTING WITH A RIFLE."

—Ernest Hemingway, 1934

12 ft 8 in (3.9 m) MARLIN
The largest caught off Cuba on rod and reel at the time

THE BIG FIVE:

Hemingway travelled to Africa in 1933 to target larger prey. The big five – lion, leopard, buffalo, rhino and elephant – were the pinnacle of hunting in these pre-conservation times. While Hemingway was a keen hunter, he showed no interest in elephants, asserting that they were, "Too important, too noble."

HONORARY GAME WARDEN OF KENYA

Awarded to Hemingway in 1954

54 SWORDFISH

Caught in one trip over three months

BLUEFIN TUNA

Hemingway prevented apple-coring – sharks taking chunks from fish while on the line – by firing his machine gun into the water

147 TROUT

Caught in a single day

HEMINGWAY'S BOAT

In 1934, on their way home from Africa to Key West, Florida, the Hemingways met the editor of *Esquire* magazine, Arnold Gingrich, in New York. After arranging for an advance of $3,000 against future articles, Hemingway promptly used the money as a down-payment on a fishing yacht from the Wheeler Shipyard in Coney Island, New York. Hemingway chartered the boat, named *Pilar*, to Miami, Florida, and on to the Caribbean. *Pilar* would become his sanctuary. For the next 26 years, during both his success and tragic decline, the boat was the one constant in his life. Upon his death, Hemingway bequeathed *Pilar* to his first mate, Gregorio Fuentes, who was the inspiration for the lead character in *The Old Man and the Sea*.

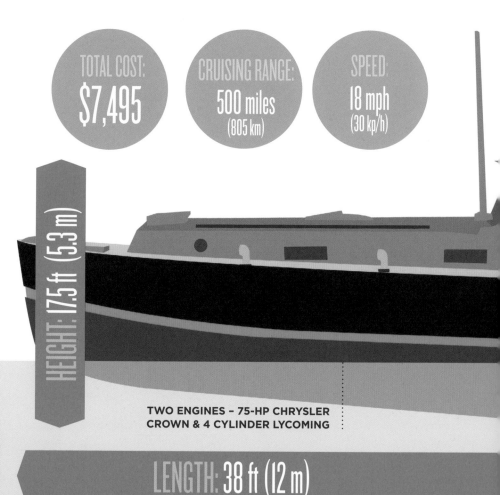

TOTAL COST: $7,495

CRUISING RANGE: 500 miles (805 km)

SPEED: 18 mph (30 kp/h)

HEIGHT: 17.5 ft (5.3 m)

TWO ENGINES – 75-HP CHRYSLER CROWN & 4 CYLINDER LYCOMING

LENGTH: 38 ft (12 m)

KEY PARTS OF THE HEMINGWAY LEGEND GREW FROM HIS TIME ON PILAR:

After spending many hours in the sun, Hemingway grew his (now iconic) beard to prevent sore skin.

During the Second World War, Hemingway armed himself with a Thompson sub-machine gun and grenades and patrolled the waters around Cuba on the hunt for German U-boats.

Trying to gun down a shark, Hemingway slipped and accidentally shot himself in both legs.

FLYING BRIDGE WITH STEERING/ CONTROL STATION

6 BUNKS

WOODEN ROLLER TO HAUL IN FISH

DOUBLE RUDDERS

CUBA!

Hemingway spent the summer of 1932 in Cuba, enjoying the serenity of the island. In 1940 he made the move permanently, at a time when the country was going through a period of political progress. Home was a large plantation on the hills overlooking Havana, known as Finca Vigía (Lookout Farm). Hemingway found life in Cuba very comfortable. He wrote prolifically and adeptly – both *For Whom the Bell Tolls* and *The Old Man and the Sea* were penned here – and he became a fixture in Havana. In 1953, a young revolutionary called Fidel Castro began a political uprising that would become the Cuban Revolution, and while relations between the USA and Cuba began to deteriorate, Hemingway stayed and supported Castro. After 20 happy years, in 1960, Hemingway departed Cuba for the US for reasons unclear. He never returned, but would always refer to himself as a 'Cubano Sato', an ordinary Cuban.

FINCA VIGÍA FACTS

12 miles (19km) outside Havana

15 acres (6 ha) of farmland

The house was rented first for

$100 per month

Hemingway purchased Finca Vigía in 1940 for

$12,500

The library today contains more than

9,000 books

On the walls are paintings by Joan Miró, Juan Gris and Georges Braque (below).

HAVANA

Cuba's largest marina is named after the author. Marina Hemingway can accommodate:

400 BOATS

A statue of Hemingway at the marina was created from melted-down boat propellers.

Hemingway dedicated his Nobel Prize to the fishermen of Cojímar, a village to the east of Havana, and he donated the gold medal to the patron saint of Cuba in the church of Our Lady of Charity. In 1986, the medal was stolen, but after an ultimatum from Raul Castro it was quickly returned.

HOTEL AMBOS MUNDOS

Hemingway's first accommodation in Havana; he stayed frequently between 1932 and 1940.

At a cost of	He stayed in Room
$1.50	**511**
per night	which is now a museum

47

PAMPLONA

SPAIN

PAMPLONA:
THE RUNNING OF THE BULLS

01

CALLE DE SANTO DOMINGO

02

CALLE MERCADERES

15 DEATHS SINCE 1924

BULL SPEED: 15 – 35 mph
(24 – 56 km/h)

BULL WEIGHT: **1,300 lb**
(600 kg)

HEMINGWAY

Hemingway first attended the Running of the Bulls at the Festival of San Fermin in 1923. Writing in the *Toronto Star Weekly*, he was enamoured of the festival: "Music was pounding and throbbing. Fireworks were being set off... All the carnivals I had ever seen paled down in comparison." The experience had such an impact on him that he returned to the festival eight times, in 1924, 1925, 1926, 1927, 1929, 1931, 1953 and 1959. But despite being notoriously adventurous, Hemingway never participated in the bull run. After his third trip, Hemingway began work on his first novel, *The Sun Also Rises*, which he based on his experiences in Pamplona that year. It made Hemingway an overnight sensation, and introduced the world to the Spanish city and bull running. His 1932 book *Death in the Afternoon*, also inspired by his time in Spain, is widely regarded as one the finest books on bullfighting.

**START:
8am**

NUMBER OF RUNNERS: 3,000

CALLE DE LA ESTAFETA

03

**AVERAGE TIME:
4 mins**

OUTFIT
- white trousers
- white shirt
- red bandana worn around neck or waist

**2,700 ft
(826 m) LONG**

**TELEFÓNICA
AND CALLEJÓN**

04

WORLD

49

RAISING THE BAR

It is no secret that Hemingway enjoyed a drink. Having started at the tender age of 15, by 19 he was indulging heavily on a daily basis. The trauma of war and the effect of living in a lively and sociable city only added to his consumption. In 1942, while living in Havana, Hemingway polished off 17 double frozen daiquiris, known as the Papa Doble, in one sitting. Similar binges happened often and by 1950, with his health in decline, he was instructed to cut out alcohol entirely. What Hemingway took this to mean was reducing his daily intake to a litre of wine and cocktails. Although he could – and often did – work his way through bottles of champagne, gin and vermouth, Hemingway's favourite tipple was just a simple scotch and soda.

F. SCOTT FITZGERALD

J. R. R. TOLKIEN

MINT JULEP

WILLIAM FAULKNER

MARTINI

E. B. WHITE

MARGARITA

JACK KEROUAC

OSCAR WILDE

DYLAN THOMAS

MAYA ANGELOU

FAVOURITE TIPPLES OF LITERARY GREATS

SCREWDRIVER

TRUMAN CAPOTE

SCOTCH

HUNTER S. THOMPSON

SCOTCH & SODA

ERNEST HEMINGWAY

HEMINGWAY

HEMINGWAY CATS

Hemingway had an affinity for cats and kept dozens of them at his Cuban estate. While living in Key West, Florida, a ship's captain offered him a cat with six toes called Snowball. The condition is caused by a genetic anomaly known as polydactylism. Today, there are 54 polydactyl cats descended from Snowball roaming the grounds of the Hemingway House Museum in Florida. The cats are protected and cared for under the terms of Hemingway's will. In 2017, Hurricane Irma struck the island, and while Key West residents were ordered to leave, employees at the museum stayed to care for the animals. The building and the cats survived unscathed.

THERE ARE 54 SIX-TOED CATS AT THE HEMINGWAY HOUSE MUSEUM

NORMAL CAT

POLYDACTYL CAT

5 FACTS ABOUT HEMINGWAY

BOXING

In his younger years, Hemingway was a successful amateur boxer. In later life, he built a boxing ring in the garden of his Key West home. He was known to tell countless boxing tales and also taught poet Ezra Pound to box.

FBI

TOP SECRET

In the 1940s, J. Edgar Hoover, head of the FBI, placed Hemingway under surveillance due to his choice to move to Cuba. He was suspected of gun running and providing information to the Loyalists in Cuba, and was also courted by the Russians.

60th BIRTHDAY

Hemingway's 60th birthday was an extravagant affair. Held in Spain over two days, the champagne was flown in from France and the food from England. There were flamenco dancers, carnival booths and a live orchestra. Guests included Italian royalty and the Maharajah of Cooch Behar (India). The firework display was so overblown that it set fire to a nearby palm tree.

CRITICAL SITUATION

In 1937, author Max Eastman wrote an unfavourable review of *Death in the Afternoon*, including the line: "Come out from behind that false hair on your chest, Ernest." Feeling that his masculinity was being questioned, Hemingway stormed into his office and demanded that both remove their shirts to see who had more chest hair. When Eastman refused, Hemingway slapped him in the face with a copy of the book.

REWRITES

In a 1958 interview with *The Paris Review*, Hemingway confessed to having rewritten the ending to *A Farewell to Arms* "39 times before I was satisfied". However, after his death, it was discovered that there were in fact 47 different endings.

ERNEST HEMINGWAY

03
WORK

"I decided that I
about each thing

ould write one story
  knew about."

ERNEST WORK

Hemingway's first book, a collection of short stories and poems, was published in 1923, when he was 24 years old. He continued to write short stories and poetry throughout his life, but it was his novels and works of non-fiction that made his name. In his 20s and 30s, Hemingway wrote with ease, but as his mental and physical health began to decline, so did his output. His family published a number of his works after his death.

1950 1949 1948 1947 1946 1945 1944 1943 1942

1951

Across the River and into the Trees

The Old Man and the Sea

1952 1953 1954 1955 1956 1957 1958 1959 1960

The Snows of Kilimanjaro and Other Stories

The Garden of Eden *The Dangerous Summer*

1988 1987 1986 1985 1984 1983 1982 1981 1980

Dateline: Toronto

1989

1990 1991 1992 1993 1994 1995 1996 1997 1998

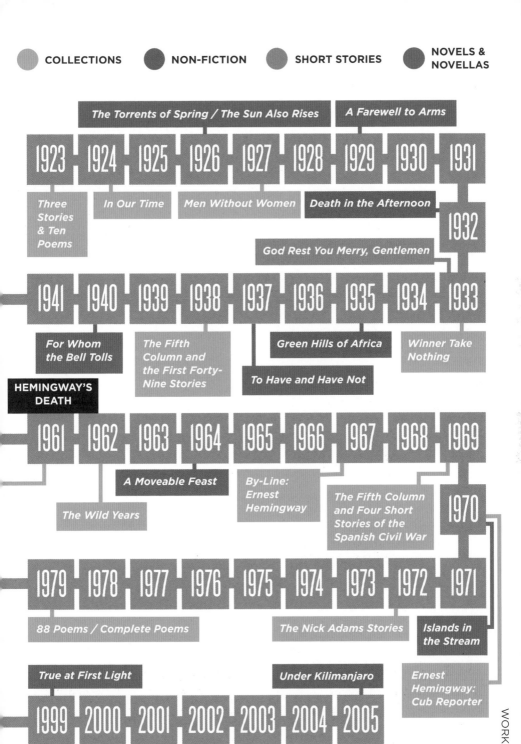

COLLECTIONS • NON-FICTION • SHORT STORIES • NOVELS & NOVELLAS

The Torrents of Spring / The Sun Also Rises

A Farewell to Arms

1923 1924 1925 1926 1927 1928 1929 1930 1931

Three Stories & Ten Poems

In Our Time

Men Without Women

Death in the Afternoon

1932

God Rest You Merry, Gentlemen

1941 1940 1939 1938 1937 1936 1935 1934 1933

For Whom the Bell Tolls

The Fifth Column and the First Forty-Nine Stories

Green Hills of Africa

Winner Take Nothing

To Have and Have Not

HEMINGWAY'S DEATH

1961 1962 1963 1964 1965 1966 1967 1968 1969

A Moveable Feast

By-Line: Ernest Hemingway

The Fifth Column and Four Short Stories of the Spanish Civil War

1970

The Wild Years

1979 1978 1977 1976 1975 1974 1973 1972 1971

88 Poems / Complete Poems

The Nick Adams Stories

Islands in the Stream

True at First Light

Under Kilimanjaro

Ernest Hemingway: Cub Reporter

1999 2000 2001 2002 2003 2004 2005

KEY WORK: THE SUN ALSO RISES

Hemingway's first novel is based on his trips to Pamplona and recounts the experiences of a group of British and American expatriates as they journey to the Festival of San Fermin in northern Spain. As they enjoy the festivities, the drinking and debauchery escalates and their complicated relationships begin to unravel. The novel captured the post-war disillusionment felt by the youth in Paris at the time. The book was well received by critics who noted Hemingway's ability to describe vivid scenes in few words, and his brilliant dialogue. However, it was dismissed by his friends and family – Hemingway's mother disliked it so much she claimed that her son was "prostituting a great talent" and "pandering to sensationalism". The novel has since been recognized as one of Hemingway's most significant works and the epitome of his unique writing style.

ERNEST HEMINGWAY

THE SUN ALSO RISES

WRITTEN:
1925 – 1926

PUBLISHED:
22 OCTOBER 1926

PUBLISHER:
SCRIBNER'S, NEW YORK

"ONE GENERATION PASSETH AWAY, AND ANOTHER GENERATION COMETH: BUT THE EARTH ABIDETH FOR EVER. THE SUN ALSO ARISETH, AND THE SUN GOETH DOWN, AND HASTETH TO HIS PLACE WHERE HE AROSE."

The title is taken from a verse in the Bible. It was intended to offer optimism to those that felt lost – "Though everything seems hopeless, the sun will rise again tomorrow".

FIRST PRINT RUN:

5,090

CHAPTERS:

19

ORIGINAL PRICE:

$2

THEMES:

- THE LOST GENERATION
- MALE INSECURITY
- SEX & LOVE
- SPORT
- NATURE
- IDENTITY
- RELIGION

ADAPTATIONS:

- FILM (1957, 1984)
- OPERA (2000)
- PLAY (2010)
- BALLET (2013)

KEY LINE:

"YOU ARE ALL A LOST GENERATION."

SETTING: SPAIN & FRANCE

IMAGERY & SYMBOLISM: BULLS AND BULL FIGHTING

53

Place on *The Guardian's* 100 Best Novels

KEY ELEMENT: ALCOHOL

All but one of the characters drink excessively. Used as a form of escapism, alcohol allows the characters to shun responsibility for their actions and avoid addressing the real issues in their relationships.

ERNEST HEMINGWAY

Having first met in Paris in 1925, Hemingway and F. Scott Fitzgerald quickly became friends. While Fitzgerald was an established novelist, Hemingway was still relatively unknown, yet it was he who was more dominant in the relationship. Often very negative in his critique of the work of others, Hemingway read and enjoyed Fitzgerald's *The Great Gatsby*. But, after Fitzgerald sent Hemingway 10 pages of edits to his draft of *A Farewell to Arms*, the relationship began to sour.

61

MARRIAGE

CHILDREN

WARTIME

Ambulance driver in WWI; war reporter in WWII

ICONIC WORK

The Old Man and the Sea (1952)

WRITING STYLE

- Short sentences
- Gritty language, direct structure
- Autobiographical

BORN

Oak Park, Illinois, USA

ERNEST HEMINGWAY (1899 – 1961)

F. SCOTT FITZGERALD

44

After 1926, the two writers rarely saw each other, and Hemingway began to publicly mock Fitzgerald, later affirming that James Joyce was the only living writer he ever respected. Fitzgerald, on the other hand, continued to refer to Hemingway as the "greatest living writer of our time". By the late 1930s, Fitzgerald's star was fading while Hemingway was at his peak, although both men struggled with alcohol addiction and health problems. In 1940, Hemingway sent Fitzgerald a copy of *For Whom the Bell Tolls*, inscribed: "To Scott with affection and esteem," Fitzgerald replied that it was, "Better than anyone else writing could do." Less than two months later, Fitzgerald suffered a fatal heart attack.

F. SCOTT FITZGERALD (1896 – 1940)

MARRIAGE

CHILDREN

WARTIME
Joined US army in 1917, never deployed.

ICONIC WORK
The Great Gatsby (1925)

WRITING STYLE
- Complex sentences
- Flowery descriptive language
- Autobiographical

BORN
Milan, Ohio, USA

KEY WORK: FOR WHOM THE BELL TOLLS

For Whom the Bell Tolls was written in various locations including Havana, Florida, Idaho and New York City. Published in October 1940, the book was an instant success and sold more than half a million copies in five months. Like his previous works, it drew on Hemingway's own experiences – specifically the Spanish Civil War. The novel is set over a 72-hour period and tells the story of an American professor who joins a band of Spanish guerrillas in the fight against the Nationalist regime. It is both a love story and a tragedy. Written in Hemingway's distinctive style – succinct prose in the third person – and interspersed with flashbacks, it presents an honest portrayal of the cruelty of war. Nominated for the Pulitzer Prize, *For Whom the Bell Tolls* was a literary triumph, and, unsurprisingly, was banned in Spain during the Nationalist regime from 1939 to 1975.

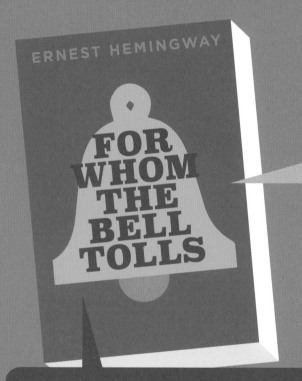

ERNEST HEMINGWAY

FOR WHOM THE BELL TOLLS

WRITTEN:
1939–1940

PUBLISHED:
21 OCTOBER 1940

PUBLISHER:
SCRIBNER'S, NEW YORK

The title is taken from John Donne's 1624 book *Devotions Upon Emergent Occasions:* "No man is an island entire of itself; every man is a piece of the continent, a part of the main; if a clod be washed away by the sea, Europe is the less, as well as if a promontory were, as well as any manner of thy friends or of thine own were; any man's death diminishes me, because I am involved in mankind. And therefore never send to know for whom the bell tolls; it tolls for thee."

FIRST PRINT RUN:
75,000

CHAPTERS:
43

PRICE:
$2.75

THEMES:

- DEATH
- FEAR
- TRAGEDY
- LOVE
- WAR
- VALUE OF HUMAN LIFE
- LOSS OF INNOCENCE

IMAGERY & SYMBOLISM:

RABBITS & HARES

AUTOMATIC WEAPONS

KEY LINE:
"THE WORLD IS A FINE PLACE AND WORTH THE FIGHTING FOR."

ADAPTATIONS:

- FILM (1943)
- TELEVISION (1959, 1965, 2012)
- MUSICAL (1978)
- SONG (1984)
- RADIO (2016)
- BALLET (2013)

8
Place on *Le Monde's* 100 Books of the Century

SETTING:

SPANISH MOUNTAINS

KEY ELEMENT: NATURE

The juxtaposition between nature and society is illustrated by the destructive nature of Man (war) versus the peace in nature (mountains and forests). The pine forests offer an escape from reality, and it is here that Jordan's romance with Maria develops: love in a time of war.

WORK

WRITE LIKE HEMINGWAY

After high school, Hemingway's first job was at the *Kansas City Star* newspaper. It was an important period in his life and the short, declarative prose that became a hallmark of his writing was adopted from the paper's style guide. The antithesis to writers such as William Faulkner, who wrote complex and colourful sentences, Hemingway had a background that steered him to write honest stories that could be read and enjoyed by the masses. Drawing on his own experiences, he produced gritty work that reflected the mood of the time. Hemingway's aptitude for creating concise and evocative prose was unparalleled, and resulted in him winning the Nobel Prize in Literature for, "The influence that he has exerted on contemporary style." Here are some ways to write like Hemingway:

ICEBERG THEORY

As he wrote, Hemingway set about describing only 10 to 20 per cent of a story and removed anything non-essential from the narrative. What remained, he argued, created a stronger prose. He compared this to an iceberg: "The dignity of movement of an ice-berg is due to only one-eighth of it being above water." He was the master of omission.

Hemingway's minimalist approach also applied to his sentences. He avoided flowery adjectives and put emphasis on verbs and nouns. The first line of the *Kansas City Star* Style Guide – Hemingway's Bible – read as follows:

"USE SHORT SENTENCES. USE SHORT FIRST PARAGRAPHS. USE VIGOROUS ENGLISH. BE POSITIVE, NOT NEGATIVE."

WRITE STANDING UP

Hemingway dedicated a room in his house to writing, but, more often than not, he would be found standing in the corner of a bedroom, his typewriter set atop of a pile of books. His reasoning: "Writing and travel broaden your ass if not your mind and I like to write standing up."

WRITE WITH A PENCIL

Hemingway believed in writing first drafts in pencil as, "you get three different sights at it to see if the reader is getting what you want him to. First when you read it over; then when it is typed you get another chance to improve it, and again in the proof." On a good day, he could exhaust at least seven pencils.

WRITE SOBER

Given his drinking habits, it's unsurprising that Hemingway's literature is littered with references to alcohol. But, while he wrote about drinking, he never drank when writing. "The only time it isn't good for you is when you write or when you fight," he once said.

IF ALL ELSE FAILS... TRY THE HEMINGWAY APP

The Hemingway Editor, developed in 2013, allows users to input their text, which it then analyzes. Hemingway-esque edits are then applied. According to the site, it: "makes your writing bold and clear... It makes sure that your reader will focus on your message, not your prose."

"WRITE ONE TRUE SENTENCE. WRITE THE TRUEST SENTENCE THAT YOU KNOW."

—Hemingway's suggestion to overcome writer's block

KEY WORK: THE OLD MAN AND THE SEA

Often cited as one of the seminal works of the 20th century, Hemingway's final novel is his most straightforward. At just over 100 pages in length, the tale of Santiago, an elderly Cuban fisherman, is honest and easy to read. Santiago's epic three-day battle with an enormous blue marlin is also a battle against poverty, loneliness and mortality, as well as an attempt to maintain his pride and re-establish his reputation as a fisherman. As Hemingway had spent the previous 10 years out of favour, and many felt that he was finished as a writer, *The Old Man and the Sea* was as much Hemingway's battle as it was Santiago's. It was originally published in *Life* magazine and sold more than five million copies in the first two days of release, before being published as a book. Despite initially receiving mixed reactions, it won both the Pulitzer Prize in 1953 and the Nobel Prize in Literature in 1954, and reinvigorated Hemingway's literary reputation.

ERNEST HEMINGWAY

THE OLD MAN AND THE SEA

WRITTEN:
1951

PUBLISHED:
8 SEPTEMBER 1952

PUBLISHER:
SCRIBNER'S,
NEW YORK

The title's simplicity provides an indication of the book's subject matter, while alluding to the idea that it is more than just a man catching a fish.

FIRST PRINT RUN:

50,000

CHAPTERS:

5

PRICE:

$3

SETTING:

HAVANA, CUBA

THEMES:

- PERSEVERANCE
- CIRCLE OF LIFE
- PAIN & SUFFERING
- HOPE
- MAN VERSUS NATURE

IMAGERY & SYMBOLISM:

Hemingway claimed there was no symbolism in the book.

ADAPTATIONS:

- FILM (1958, 1999)
- TELEVISION (1990)
- ANIMATED FILM (2000)
- PLAY (2010)

KEY LINE:
"LET HIM THINK THAT I AM MORE MAN THAN I AM AND I WILL BE SO."

CHARACTERS:

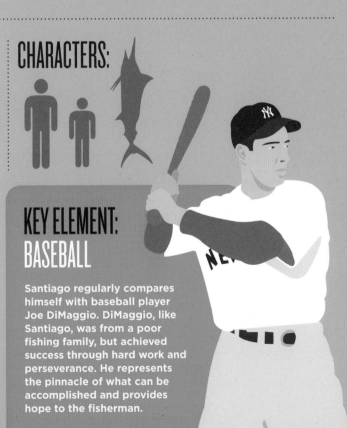

KEY ELEMENT:
BASEBALL

Santiago regularly compares himself with baseball player Joe DiMaggio. DiMaggio, like Santiago, was from a poor fishing family, but achieved success through hard work and perseverance. He represents the pinnacle of what can be accomplished and provides hope to the fisherman.

PRIZEWINNER!

In 1953, Hemingway was awarded the Pulitzer Prize for Fiction, an honour that many felt was long overdue. Twelve years earlier, *For Whom the Bell Tolls* was advocated by the Pulitzer Fiction Committee, but was rejected by the board because they felt that its "faults partly outweigh its merits". Instead they chose not to recognize any work that year. After the Pulitzer Prize, other awards quickly followed, including the American Academy of Arts and Letters Award of Merit and the ultimate accolade, the Nobel Prize in Literature. Hemingway had achieved what every artist strives for – commercial and now critical success.

1921

SILVER MEDAL OF MILITARY VALOR

For: Acts of heroism in the First World War

1941

GOLD MEDAL FROM THE LIMITED EDITIONS CLUB

For: *For Whom the Bell Tolls*

1953

PULITZER PRIZE FOR FICTION

For: "Distinguished fiction published in book form during the year by an American author, preferably dealing with American life"

1954

AMERICAN ACADEMY OF ARTS AND LETTERS AWARD OF MERIT

For: Acknowledgement of his career (came with a prize of $1,000)

1947

BRONZE STAR MEDAL

For: War reporting in the Second World War

1948

ORDER OF MERIT OF THE ITALIAN REPUBLIC

For: "Contributing blood and money to the Italian soil"

1952

CUBAN MEDAL OF HONOR

For: "In the name of the professional marlin fisherman"

1954

ORDER OF CARLOS MANUEL DE CÉSPEDES

For: The highest civilian award in Cuba (reason not given)

1954

NOBEL PRIZE IN LITERATURE

For: "His mastery of the art of narrative, most recently demonstrated in *The Old Man and the Sea,* and for the influence that he has exerted on contemporary style"

1955

ORDER OF SAN CRISTÓBAL

For: Recognition of his interest in Cuba

THE LOST SUITCASE

In 1922, Hemingway was in Lausanne, Switzerland, on assignment for the *Toronto Star Weekly*. His then-wife Hadley remained in Paris, but was due to join him, so that they could go skiing in the Alps. Under Hemingway's instruction, Hadley packed a suitcase of all of his writings and short stories over the previous three years, as well as the draft for his first novel, and headed for the Gare de Lyon. After loading her belongings onto the train, Hadley went to buy a newspaper and bottle of water. However, when she returned to the train, she suddenly realized that the suitcase had been stolen. Hemingway was, at the time, an unpublished author, and the loss caused him great distress. Though he never continued writing the lost 'first' novel, less than four years later he was a household name.

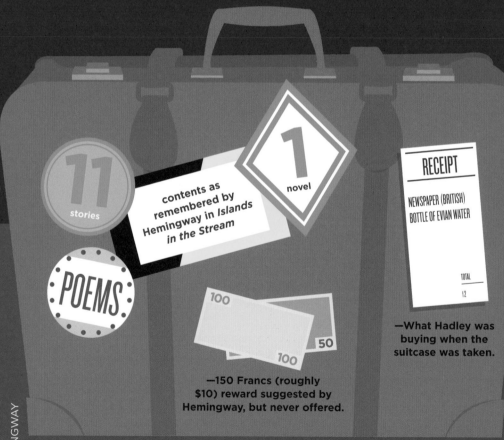

11 stories

contents as remembered by Hemingway in *Islands in the Stream*

1 novel

POEMS

100
100
50

—150 Francs (roughly $10) reward suggested by Hemingway, but never offered.

RECEIPT

NEWSPAPER (BRITISH)
BOTTLE OF EVIAN WATER

TOTAL

12

—What Hadley was buying when the suitcase was taken.

In typical Hemingway fashion, the incident also made an appearance in *A Moveable Feast*, but with his reaction to the loss toned down somewhat.

ERNEST HEMINGWAY

04
LEGACY

"PROBABLY NO OTHER AMERICAN WRITER OF OUR TIME HAS SET SUCH A STAMP ON MODERN LITERATURE. HEMINGWAY WAS ONE OF OUR TRUE POETS."

—Alfred Kazin, American writer and critic, *New York Times*, 1961

LITERARY INFLUENCE

JACK KEROUAC
1922–69

Novelist, poet
and father of the
Beat movement

Hemingway influence:
The Beat Generation were
the Lost Generation of
the 1950s, and Kerouac's
autobiographical work
shared thematic similarities
with Hemingway's. His
writing was a reaction to
events of the time and,
like Ernest, he wrote about
alcohol just as much as he
consumed it.

Key work:
ON THE ROAD
(1957)

HUNTER S. THOMPSON
1937–2005

Journalist and author
who founded the Gonzo
journalism movement

Hemingway influence:
Thompson idolized
Hemingway and once
typed out the entirety
of *A Farewell to Arms*
to learn to write like his
hero. In a 1964 visit to
Hemingway's Idaho house,
Thompson stole a set of
antlers off the wall and
in 2005, like his idol, he
committed suicide.

Key work:
***FEAR AND
LOATHING
IN LAS VEGAS***
(1971)

J. D. SALINGER
1919–2010

American novelist and
short story writer

Hemingway influence:
Salinger is recognized
for his direct prose and
mastery of narration,
and for his depiction of
post-war life – all things
said about Hemingway
previously.In a letter
between the two men,
Salinger admitted to being
the, "National chairman of
the Hemingway Fan Clubs."

Key work:
***THE CATCHER
IN THE RYE***
(1951)

Hemingway was one of the most influential writers of the 20th century, and his impact on literature is still evident. He built a reputation with short stories, and his direct style of storytelling became the model for literature in the 1930s, opening a whole generation to the idea it wasn't essential to write lengthy prose to create a captivating story. In the years that followed, both stylistically and thematically he was copied by writers such as Raymond Chandler and Albert Camus and indirectly influenced a host of others, including Chuck Palahniuk and Bret Easton Ellis. Here are some writers whose work would not have happened in the way it did without Hemingway.

GABRIEL GARCÍA MÁRQUEZ
1927–2014

Colombian writer and winner of the 1982 Nobel Prize in Literature

Hemingway influence: Heavily critical of Colombian and foreign politics, his conservative style was taken from Hemingway as much as from his journalistic background. He admired Hemingway's spirit and applied the 'iceberg theory' when composing his novels.

Key work:

***ONE HUNDRED YEARS OF SOLITUDE* (1967)**

RAY BRADBURY
1920–2002

American author and screenwriter

Hemingway influence: Bradbury wrote many short stories, featuring Hemingway in two of them. Also hailing from Chicago, he openly admitted to being influenced by Hemingway and went to the printing plant to get an early copy of *The Old Man and The Sea* to read with friends.

Key work:

***FAHRENHEIT 451* (1953)**

ELMORE LEONARD
1925–2013

American novelist, short story writer and screenwriter

Hemingway influence: Leonard's first writings were short stories but he found success through his novels, influenced by the work of Hemingway. "I learned by imitating Hemingway," Leonard once said, and commended him for, "Making writing look easy."

Key work:

***GET SHORTY* (1990)**

FIRST EDITIONS

In the 50 years since his death, Hemingway memorabilia has become increasingly valuable, with many photos, letters and his personal effects having gone under the hammer. In 2004, a first edition of his 1926 novel *The Sun Also Rises*, limited to only 5,090 copies, realized $366,400 at Sotheby's New York – a record for the author. So how does he compare to his contemporaries at auction?

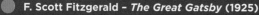

- Virginia Woolf – *Mrs Dalloway* (1925)
- Ezra Pound – *A Lume Spento* (1908)
- T. E. Lawrence – *Seven Pillars of Wisdom* (1926)
- Joseph Conrad – *Nostromo* (1904)
- J. D. Salinger – *The Catcher in the Rye* (1951)
- William Faulkner – *Absalom, Absalom!* (1936)
- George Orwell – *1984* (1949)
- ERNEST HEMINGWAY – *THE SUN ALSO RISES* (1926)
- F. Scott Fitzgerald – *The Great Gatsby* (1925)
- James Joyce – *Ulysses* (1922)

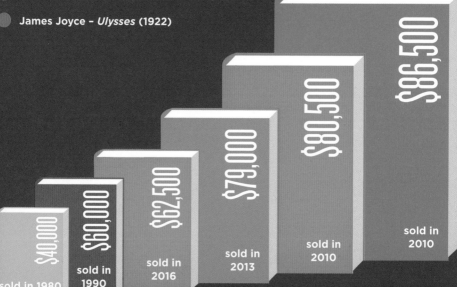

$40,000 — sold in 1980

$60,000 — sold in 1990

$62,500 — sold in 2016

$79,000 — sold in 2013

$80,500 — sold in 2010

$86,500 — sold in 2010

$210,000

sold in
2013

$366,400

sold in
2004

$377,000

sold in
2017

$460,000

sold in
2009

The copy of *The Sun Also Rises* sold at auction in 2004 was inscribed to the doctor who delivered two of Hemingway's children.

ERNEST HEMINGWAY HOME & MUSEUM

FLORIDA

KEY WEST

OWNED BY HEMINGWAY:

1931–61

3,000 ft^2 (279 m^2)

LARGEST SINGLE RESIDENTIAL PROPERTY ON KEY WEST

At the suggestion of friend and novelist John Dos Passos, in 1928 Ernest and wife Pauline left Europe and headed to Key West, Florida. For the next three years, they rented various properties on the island, until 1931 when – as a belated wedding present – Pauline's uncle purchased the house at 907 Whitehead Street, in the heart of the old town. The house, built in 1851 in a colonial style, had been neglected, so Hemingway spent the next eight years restoring it to its former glory and thereby making it the ideal setting for his most prolific period of writing. Hemingway left Florida in 1939, but retained the property until his death, when it was sold off. It was declared a US National Historic Landmark on 24 November 1968, and is now a privately owned museum dedicated to the man himself.

$20,000
Cost to install a swimming pool in the garden. It was the first pool on Key West.

MOVIE LOCATION
In 1988, the house was used during the filming of the James Bond film *Licence to Kill*.

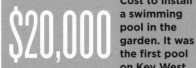
PURCHASED FOR: $8,000
SOLD FOR: $80,000

URINAL IN THE GARDEN:

Stolen by Hemingway from his favourite bar, Sloppy Joe's. His reasoning: he'd "pissed away" so much money, he now owned it.

PRICELESS ART:
Art on the walls by friends such as Joan Miró, Henry Faulkner and Pablo Picasso.

A LENGTHY SENTENCE

Literature at the end of the 19th century was changing. Romanticism had been dropped in favour of realism, but the Victorian style of writing – with complex, often flowery, prose – was still very much in vogue. Some authors, such as Charles Dickens, had their work published in serial form and were paid by the word. Dickens' work was highly descriptive, and he used ornate language, repetition and lists to shape his stories. When Hemingway's work first appeared in the 1920s, it was shockingly different. Utilizing his journalism background, where space was limited and clarity was key, he told stories with short, suggestive sentences. With an average sentence length of just eight words, his aim was, "To put down on paper what I see and what I feel in the best and simplest way." Hemingway developed a unique voice – one that has often been copied, but never equalled.

417
WORDS

Not every Hemingway sentence was short, with his longest sentence appearing in *Green Hills of Africa*.

LONG SENTENCES IN LITERATURE:

1,289 words
ABSALOM, ABSALOM!
WILLIAM FAULKNER (1936)

4,391 words
ULYSSES
JAMES JOYCE (1922)

13,955 words
THE ROTTERS' CLUB
JONATHAN COE (2001)

THE WORLD RECORD IS 150,000 WORDS *ZONE* MATHIAS ENARD (2008)

AVERAGE WORDS PER SENTENCE

23 "BUT HE WAS NOW MARRIED; AND SHE CONDEMNED HER HEART FOR THE LURKING FLATTERY WHICH SO MUCH HEIGHTENED THE PAIN OF THE INTELLIGENCE."

22 "IT IS THE EASIEST THING IN THE WORLD FOR A MAN TO LOOK AS IF HE HAD A GREAT SECRET IN HIM."

17 "THAT GLORIOUS VISION OF DOING GOOD IS SO OFTEN THE SANGUINE MIRAGE OF SO MANY GOOD MINDS."

16 "THERE IS ALWAYS MORE MISERY AMONG THE LOWER CLASSES THAN THERE IS HUMANITY IN THE HIGHER."

18 "THE HATTER'S REMARK SEEMED TO HAVE NO SORT OF MEANING IN IT, AND YET IT WAS CERTAINLY ENGLISH."

15 "THEY CAN ONLY SEE THE MERE SHOW, AND NEVER CAN TELL WHAT IT REALLY MEANS."

14 "SO WE BEAT ON, BOATS AGAINST THE CURRENT, BORNE BACK CEASELESSLY INTO THE PAST."

8 "EVERYONE GIVEN THE RIGHT OPPORTUNITY WILL BEHAVE BADLY."

1811	1851	1859	1862	1865	1899	1925	1926
Jane Austen *Sense and Sensibility*	**Herman Melville** *Moby Dick*	**Charles Dickens** *A Tale of Two Cities*	**Victor Hugo** *Les Miserables*	**Lewis Carroll** *Alice's Adventures in Wonderland*	**Joseph Conrad** *Heart of Darkness*	**F. Scott Fitzgerald** *The Great Gatsby*	**Ernest Hemingway** *The Sun Also Rises*

THE MAN, THE MYTH

Hemingway often spoke about writing truthfully. In *A Farewell to Arms*, he summarizes that, "A writer's job is to tell the truth," and in *A Moveable Feast*, he declares, "All you have to do is write one true sentence. Write the truest sentence that you know." Hemingway did not live by these words. As a storyteller he was guilty of exaggeration, both in his writing and in his personal life. In his non-fiction work and newspaper articles, he allowed artistic licence to enrich the narrative. When recounting past situations, Hemingway would embellish the truth so often it's impossible to distinguish between fact and fiction. While it's true he lived a remarkable life, a whole host of anecdotes have been associated with Hemingway, purely because it doesn't seem completely ridiculous. Here are just some of the Hemingway myths:

THE SIX-WORD STORY

"For Sale: baby shoes, never worn." Hemingway penned this six-word story on a restaurant napkin for a bet.

The real source of the six-word story dates back to 1906, when an advert appeared in a local paper: "For sale, baby carriage, never been used. Apply at this office".

NATIVE AMERICAN HERITAGE

In a 1949 letter, Hemingway wrote that he had "a Cheyenne great-great grandmother" and at other times referred to his father's "Indian blood".

There is no evidence to support this, and instead it appears that Hemingway was trying to undermine his white middle-class upbringing.

STARVING IN PARIS

When Hemingway first arrived in Paris, he was so poor that he resorted to eating wild pigeons that he caught by hand in the Jardin du Luxembourg.

The truth was that his wife Hadley had a decent annual income from inheritance and the dollar went a lot further in Europe.

NAZI KILLER

While working as a reporter on the frontlines in the Second World War, Hemingway wrote to friends that he'd taken to assisting in the war effort and killed a total of 122 German soldiers.

Picasso, who dined with Hemingway after the war, offered an insight: "It was a lie. Maybe he had killed plenty of wild animals, but he never killed a man. If he had killed one, he wouldn't have needed to pass around souvenirs."

LIBERATION OF PARIS

It's often reported that Hemingway was the first American in Paris during its liberation at the end of the Second World War. He also single-handedly took the Ritz from the Germans and finished off 51 drinks at the bar.

With the city already cleared, Hemingway entered with a group of US soldiers and headed straight for the empty bar at the Ritz. That he drank 51 dry martinis in one sitting is unproven.

CLAIM   FACT

THINGS NAMED AFTER HEMINGWAY

PAPA'S PILAR RUM

FURNITURE RANGE

SPINYCHEEK SCORPIONFISH

(Neomerinthe hemingwayi)

STREET IN RONDA, ANDALUCIA, SPAIN

HARDWOOD FLOORING

HOTELS & RESORTS

EYEWEAR

MINOR PLANET 3656 HEMINGWAY

COFFEE BRAND

PEN/HEMINGWAY AWARD

INTERNATIONAL IMITATION HEMINGWAY COMPETITION

SAUCES

FOUNTAIN PEN

The
HUNT
GRILLING SAUCE

MATTRESSES

UNFINISHED BUSINESS

Hemingway's last published work was written in 1951. In the decade that followed, he struggled to recapture his voice and found the process arduous. Even so, Hemingway persevered. Though he never had another book in print during his lifetime, on his death three manuscripts were discovered. Two of them, *Islands in the Stream* and *A Moveable Feast*, were both found to be complete; but *The Garden of Eden*, a project that he'd been working on since 1946, was unfinished. Originally more than 1,500 pages in length and with more than 200,000 words, in its final published state it was heavily abridged, down to just 70,000. The publishers claimed this was necessary to create a coherent story but were heavily criticized, sparking a debate regarding the legacy of a literary estate. Hemingway is not the only author to have had work published posthumously, with some more finished than others.

0%   *Percentage complete*   100%

GEOFFREY CHAUCER
THE CANTERBURY TALES
started 1387
published 1476

24 of 120 tales completed

MARQUIS DE SADE
THE 120 DAYS OF SODOM
started 1785
published 1904

Written on a 40-foot-long roll of paper

JANE AUSTEN
SANDITON
started 1817
published 1925

Died four months after writing last word

CHARLES DICKENS
THE MYSTERY OF EDWIN DROOD
started 1870
published 1870

6 of 12 instalments completed

MARK TWAIN

THE MYSTERIOUS STRANGER

started 1897
published 1916

Compiled from three unfinished manuscripts

JACK LONDON

THE ASSASSINATION BUREAU, LTD

started 1910
published 1963

Completed by American author Robert Fish

F. SCOTT FITZGERALD

THE LOVE OF THE LAST TYCOON

started 1937
published 1941

Semi-autobiographical novel

ERNEST HEMINGWAY

THE GARDEN OF EDEN

started 1946
published 1986

Written over 15 years

ALBERT CAMUS

THE LAST MAN

started 1959
published 1994

Completed by his daughter Catherine

DAVID FOSTER WALLACE

THE PALE KING

started 2000
published 2011

Committed suicide before it was complete

LEGACY

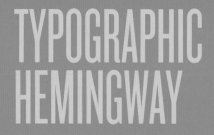

TYPOGRAPHIC
HEMINGWAY

CARIBBEAN

PAPA KETCHUM MEDAL OF VALOR

PAMPLONA SHARKS WOUNDED

FESTIVAL OF SAN FERMIN

SAFARI GERTRUDE STEIN

AUTOBIOGRAPHICAL

WAR STYLE GUIDE FIRST WORLD WAR

NOVELS POEMS SHRAPNEL ICEBERG THEORY ADVENTURE

CHICAGO FRANCE WAR TORONTO STAR

EZRA POUND ERNEST OAK PARK MARLIN ELECTROCONVULSIVE THERAPY

HEMIN

FOR WHOM THE BELL TOLLS PARIS

SPAIN SHORT SENTENCES AMBULANCE DRIVER WRITER WAR HERO ACROSS THE RIVER AND INTO THE TREES

PLANE CRASH SCHIO BOXING DEPRESSION TUNA SHORT STORIES PAPA DOBLE

SHOTGUN

LOST SUITCASE DEATH DRINKING CUBANO SATO

JOURNALIST THE OLD MAN AND THE SEA

FINCA VIGIA KANSAS CITY STAR A LOST GENERATION DEATH IN THE AFTERNOON

SUICIDE IDAHO RUNNING OF THE BULLS

BULLFIGHTING SCOTCH PILAR DISPATCHES

FIDEL CASTRO NOBEL PRIZE PULITZER PRIZE THE SUN ALSO RISES SECOND WORLD WAR

A FAREWELL TO ARMS A MOVEABLE FEAST JAMES JOYCE

GWAY HAVANA

WOUNDED SPANISH CIVIL WAR UGANDA

F SCOTT FITZGERALD INFIDELITY BESTSELLER SKIING BEARD CUBAN REVOLUTION

FOUR WIVES AFRICA INJURIES FISHING

VIOLIN HUNTING CUBA CATS LATIN QUARTER KEY WEST

TYPEWRITER FLORIDA THREE CHILDREN ALCOHOL PABLO PICASSO

NOVELIST GRITTY LANGUAGE SAILING USA THE RITZ

BIOGRAPHIES

Gertrude Stein
(1874–1946)
An American writer, poet, art buyer, mentor and patron, Stein was influential in the careers of Picasso and Matisse, amongst others. Stein moved to Paris, France, in 1903 and, for a time, was close friends with Hemingway. She was godmother to his first son, John.

James Joyce
(1882–1941)
The Irish novelist spent many nights drinking with Hemingway in Paris. He famously caused bar fights, only to hide behind his much larger friend. His novel *Ulysses* is widely regarded as one of the most important works of 20th-century literature.

Margaux Hemingway
(1954–96)
Hemingway's granddaughter was a model and actress. She was the first model to be offered a million-dollar contract. For most of her life, she suffered with mental health issues and battled addiction. Like her grandfather, she committed suicide.

Charles Scribner, Jr
(1921–95)
He was President and Chairman of Charles Scribner's Sons – Hemingway's publisher – from 1952 until 1984. During Hemingway's final years, Scribner was his personal editor and, in 1974, he edited *The Enduring Hemingway*, examining Hemingway's writings and philosophies.

Ezra Pound
(1885–1972)
An American poet, Pound was a major figure in 20th-century modernist poetry. Lifelong friends with Hemingway, he championed his work and helped edit his early writings. In 1945, he was arrested and incarcerated for 12 years on charges of treason after criticizing the US government.

Pauline Marie Pfeiffer
(1895–1951)
Hemingway's second wife was a journalist from a wealthy American family. After stints at *Vanity Fair* and *Vogue* in New York, she moved to France to write for *Vogue Paris*. She met Hemingway in 1925 and they married in 1927.

Mary Welsh
(1908–86)

An American writer and journalist, Welsh was Hemingway's fourth wife. After his death, she acted as his literary executor and oversaw the publication of a number of unfinished works. In 1976, Welsh released a book, *How It Was*, detailing her relationship with Hemingway.

F. Scott Fitzgerald
(1896–1940)

The American writer, whose work chronicled the Jazz Age, met Hemingway in a Parisian bar and the two shared a turbulent relationship. Addicted to alcohol, he suffered two heart attacks in the 1930s, before a third, fatal attack in 1940.

Maxwell Perkins
(1884–1947)

A literary editor at Charles Scribner's Sons in New York for 36 years, Perkins was responsible for signing F. Scott Fitzgerald and editing *The Great Gatsby*. He was introduced to Hemingway in 1926 and remained his editor until his death. Hemingway dedicated *The Old Man and the Sea* to him.

Martha Gellhorn
(1908–98)

Hemingway's third wife was a successful travel writer and novelist. Born in Missouri, USA, she moved to Europe in the 1930s and was one of the first female war correspondents. She committed suicide in London at the age of 89.

Elizabeth Hadley Richardson
(1891–1979)

Hemingway was just 22 when he married Hadley Richardson, who was eight years his senior. The couple moved to Paris in 1922, and had a son in 1923. After Hemingway started an affair with Pauline Pfeiffer in 1926, the couple divorced.

John Dos Passos
(1896–1970)

Passos was an American novelist and artist and was considered one of the key writers of The Lost Generation. In 1928, on Passos's recommendation, the Hemingways moved to Key West, Florida. Passos severed the friendship in 1937 over differing opinions on the Spanish Civil War.

friend
family
editor

INDEX